T0196884

sowing nightshade in the wastelands of cities

poems
by
ralph günther mohnnau

english
christopher martin

Order this book online at www.trafford.com
or email orders@trafford.com

Most Trafford titles are also available at major online book retailers.

Print information available on the last page.

ISBN: 978-1-4120-6716-4 (sc)

Trafford rev. 05/29/2020

 www.trafford.com

North America & international
toll-free: 1 888 232 4444 (USA & Canada)
fax: 812 355 4082

Ralph Günther Mohnnau...?

In the spring of 1986, theatre colleague Manuel Lütgenhorst handed me a play in need of translating. Maybe you won't like it, he said. It's poetic, even pornographic, and very German. I was intrigued.

ZEIT DER MUSCHELN (*Time of the Conch*) was poetic, yes, and erotic (but not pornographic)...and certainly more than peculiarly German. Yes, I would be delighted to tackle an English version. *CRY OF THE MANTIS* — in collaboration with Daniel Woker — was the result.

Upon its completion I met with Matthias Raue, who was commissioned to compose a score accompanying the piece, and questioned him about the mysterious Mohnnau. He laughed. You should go to Frankfurt and meet him for yourself. I did. And that was the beginning of a beautiful friendship.

As a man of the theatre — classical theatre in particular — I had a sound footing in poetry. But a collection of Mohnnau's contemporary poems published as *GAMMASTRAHLEN* (*Gamma-Rays*) moved me, making me wince and smile in a way that I would never have expected. Some day, when my German is better, I said, you have to let me get my hands on these!

Two years later, Mohnnau called me in to "doctor" a production of his *ZEIT DER MUSCHELN* in Paris that had run into technical difficulties in its use of holograms; our work together there led to an English language production at Seven Stages Performing Arts Center/Atlanta in the spring of 1990. Mohnnau turned up for the sold-out premiere, accompanied by his Spanish translator Pere Bonin, to find his play emotionally charged by seven American actresses, all of whom had fallen head-over-heels in love with the poet (in absentia).

Then the call came, asking me if I would be kind enough to look over an English translation he'd commissioned for his current collection *ICH PFLANZE TOLLKIRSCHEN IN DIE WÜSTEN DER STÄDTE*. I was deeply distressed. They were not right, not right at all. Mohnnau's poems are filled with fascinating personal imagery and humor and an unexpected eroticism you can reach out and touch. Did I have the time to re-translate them? I would make the time!

Botho Strauss, Molière, Rostand, Lorca, Strindberg — never did I have so much downright fun in threading this poet's elusive images, unraveling them and reweaving them into a parallel English. Each and every colleague I read them to, listened, nodded sagely, pricked up an ear, and (yes!) laughed outright in recognition, at Mohnnau's unique insight into humanity.

SOWING NIGHTSHADE IN THE WASTELANDS OF CITIES is a private exhibition — a collection drawn by a scintillating artist unafraid to take that step through the light — as well as dark — glass of his soul.

Ralph Günther Mohnnau...? I suggest you meet him for yourself...

Christopher Martin
New York, May 2006

cover photo
Gudrun Véckony

author photo
Jörg Poppe-Marquardt

sowing nightshade in the wastelands of cities has been published with a companion collection – *on the tidings of time* — also available from Trafford Publishing.

the master questioned his pupils:
I do not wish to know of you: how were
the fifteen days gone by, but tell me:
how will the fifteen days be to come?
no one answered.
the master himself replied:
day by day: that is the good day.

yun men wen-yen china, 900 a.d.

I

...and drunk upon kisses
　　　　　　tumbled the GODS

_____*rgm*_____

LIFE

I learned the art of arithmetics
learned the laws of arcs and angles
learned the architecture too of atoms
&
the orbits astrological
&
the cellular forms of life
in nucleae

I heard about the big bang
& that taught me the time: fourth dimension
far as we can tell

and yes I learned:
no speed is faster than the speed of light
AND: einstein $e = mc^2$

AND YET I KNEW:

these were things
as fleeting as a speck of sand
                    what counts
                            is LIVING
                                    LOVING
                                            LAUGHING

these the things
inexplicable
inadmissible
inaccessible to laser rays

that leave no trace in the cloud chamber

LIFE

life-fugue

I dreamed
     / am I dreaming
          / living
               / seeing: SEE:
backed against the shell-pocked wall of the prison/my
hands lashed fast behind me to an iron ring
      eyes bound taut in a black linen cloth

:

early morning
     four now
     perhaps even five
            sun on the rise
               and warm on my face
a single crow
no: two
cackling there in the brush
not disturbed in the least by the firing squad its
six rifles now taking aim
:
I see them
        their cordite-ringed barrels
           as they train them on me
               as they snap to attention
I see them through the dark linen cloth
           that's there to stop me from seeing
hear him
     AIM!
        the bark of the officer:
               FIRE!!!!!

:
I WATCH

as the bullets whistle into me
                    through the forehead
          to the eyes
              to the nose
          two the teeth
and wince
as they tear their way through the flesh
boring : spinning : burning
                  AND STILL!!!!!
:
THERE I STAND
          UPRIGHT
                  SIX SHOTS IN THE SKULL

still I see it: the sun
there: still squabbling as ever: the crows
now: the magpies
                  SEE THEM:
                          the death squad
                    the guardsmen
                      the chaplain
                  the captain
:
slowly
oh so slowly
          moving out toward them
while untying the blindfold
while my
        fingers pick
              six bullets
                  out of the skull
one
    after
        the
          other
            :
              striding out toward them

my killers

                    :

                    I've something you've lost
                                        I say to them &
                            hand them back one bullet each

WHAT YOU SEEK TO DESTROY
                                    smile I
WILL NEVER BE SILENCED
                        WITH BULLETS
&!
      taking my time I stroll out
                              into the orange glare of the sun
on past
              the faces of terror
&
the chatter of magpies

the corsican monk

he shuffled toward me in calvi
early one afternoon
in his maize-burnished robes
& his toes sandaled in leather
HIS FACE:
it is his face
which has etched itself in my brain
like a meteor
blasting out a crater
in the desert
THAT FACE:
the skin shimmered through
in a softened light
wavering as if
weightless
inside/out

:

clear to me / nothing could shake him
he needed no raw eggs in whiskey
no ten rounds
& moist female thighs
to be happy
nor big bang & glimpse
at the innards of atoms

the veiled light of his eyes fell on me
                as if in apology / that he shared the same
      side of the street as I
                   as we glided by one another
                               not a touch
YET SOMETHING COURSED THROUGH ME /
                         electrifying me
                  as I strayed into his field –
        for an instant
              wired directly into his circuit /
                  felt / my own cells
             energized / conducting
                 a force
             somehow transmitted
      intense & invisible
           I stood/stand/stunned/benumbed/
      surrendered helpless to the voltage
    which he'd woven round me
        like a web of fine mesh

        and then he'd already passed

:
I catch myself
wanting to follow him/wanting to question him
on the meaning of life
             on love & on death
               & where do we come from & where do we go
                 & what is it: the soul?

for a while I watch him move off
                in the sparkle of afternoon light
      till he's swallowed in the swarm
           of the crowd
   I take a deep breath
   stretch my muscles
   strain my face toward the sun
   :
   what a good day

herr von m.

his black-lacquered walking stick
        pierces the electric eye of the lift
stepping in:
                in his black serge coat
                        his black suede shoes
                                in his black felt hat with its
                black silk band
                                he looms
                                        like one chiseled rough-hewn
                                        from a shard of petrified slag

there he stands:
                        93 years/lashless/six foot one maybe two
                                his aquamarine eyes
                                                forever awash
                        black & stiff & erect
                                        the prussian officer true-blue
& when he speaks of war:
                                those were the days
                                        under barrage at verdun
                                the nerve-gas falling upon ypres
                                        when U-20 sank the LUSITANIA
                        gun-running clandestined for england /
                the wounded piled up in sick bay
                                the stench of the gangrene / my
                        lungs shattered by shrapnel
                                                :
                                        here was a guy/
                                                who spun
                                        no fairy tales

& then: africa corps
    paratroopers at crete
      stalingrad
          if we hadn't been
             ambushed by winter

:
he lived off war
& his memories of war
          the umbilical cord
       the life-giving breath/
          the res/cue/for him
       in these days
          this time of unrest
      & the fear
        of annihilation
          from nuclear ash —

he steps out at the seventh floor
    stationed in the electric eye
  as if the lift were there just for him
     no need for worry my young friend
       says he
      & his voice as dry
as the crackle of
    yesterday's bread
we shall never see another great war
there is far too much fear in the world
and fear wins nobody wars
      he smiles & steps from the electric eye
       & the door slides shut obscuring
        the figure in black

    & for an instant I have the feeling
    I should hug him

KID / here's looking at you

he had himself
one rather unorthodox death
    said the doctor
        quite ingenious
yes artistic I'd say —
            as he scribbled his signature
              to the certificate
      the piano tilted at an angle
        held there balanced on edge by
           the music stand
        before he lashed himself to the chair
you see
he had only
to lean backward a bit…
        the piano simply shattered
        the cranium
        death instantaneous I'd say
:
yes : stephan : STEPHAN:
       couldn't you come up with another out
      in respect to this life
        not so violent/and cruel
          and dramatic WITH
     :sleeping pills
     :exhaust fumes
     :deadly nightshade
      or if you'd asked me: a good shot in the mouth
        with the old smith & wesson
         sitting calm & relaxed
BUT
then you were always out of step
    one/for whom two times two is not necessarily four —
even in class
     as you laid waste to our chemistry lab
       with your lunatic formulas
         & madman's experiments
       on the verge of absolute zero
       one degree kelvin your favorite —

AND: not to forget:
>   the time old heidegger
>   was about to delve into the *unspoken/ that*
>   *lies alone in the spoken*
>   interjecting mid-sentence
>   one of those razor-sharp zaps
>   from the back of the hushed lecture hall:
>   *mistake /*
>   *herr professor*
& heidegger's response:
>   *he who thinks / mistakes not*
>   *he mis-thinks*
>   and that shut you up for awhile

:

your never-finished poem TANTALUS
>   :

>   you were a creature
>   from another galaxy
>   living off stale crusts/ thistle tea
>   & dried figs
>   & while I was plucking the pubes
>   you read plato/ goethe
>   kant & wittgenstein/ kung-futse too
>   proving with a laser's precision
>   that mind & spirit outweighed
>   a firm-nippled breast
>   & the blood of a fresh-bitten lip

:

true to yourself
>   your stale crusts/ thistle tea & dried figs
>   your philosophers/ poets
>   & ZEN masters of old
>   in that monk's cell in glottertal
>   & that broken-down bike
we'd ride reckless summers to kaiserstuhl
>   to plunder our cherries/ this
>   the one libertine indulgence allowed
>   :

WHERE ARE YOU NOW?
have you found the answer at last/*just what is: life?*
                              what: the spirit?
the never-ending discussions
that lasted till dawn

                    your flickering eyes
                        the lines of your face
                                carved in stone/
                            granite stone
                    &
                        sometimes
                                yet sometimes
                    that thin-lipped
                            arrogant
                        know-it-all
                                    smile
                        mistake –
you were not of this world
and yet/if I am to believe you/
yours/mine/our earthly lives are logged: analogued
for all time on some intangible tape
recorded
        reversed
                replayed
                    at random
for the initiated
as seeing/as knowing as you/
                        not the feeling like me
you're beyond us now/you
spirit of spirits
        on which of your seven spheres
                have you landed?
                        on that of philosophers?
                            on that of fine arts?
                    or the sixth sphere
                            of poets?

I never understood
        why were you
                so against this life on earth?
                the refreshing spray of the rain/
                    the trace of a snail in the dew/
                        the laughter of children?
                you never experienced/what it means: to love

WELL NO MATTER:
                    if it's all
                    as you said it would be
                        all those bleak brooding all-nights
                in glottertal
                        or
                    under the chirping cherry branches
                    of kaiserstuhl:
we will meet again/my friend
                        not a matter of: days/years
                    when I have shed this mortal coil
                                like a snake
                            discards its skin
no
one evening
suddenly
                    you'll stand there in my room
                                as if nothing passed
                        resume your old place in that wicker chair
&
we'll simply continue
                    picking up
                        at the point
where the two of us left off
last time

mid/NIGH/t: poem

I sit at my desk
doodling on the page whereupon
                there ought to be a poem
EVEN:
        a NON-POEM
while the lazy drizzle drums on the roof/
                        droning me asleep with its
                    steady drip/drip/drip
                        &
the teabag hanging limp in the glass
                    &
                    the neon sign opposite out for the night
        &
        while I wonder
        whether to heat more hot water or not
                    which means: off to the kitchen
            & plug in the kettle
it seems
as if someone is here in my room ------
----

        don't let me disturb you
            I hear a voice
                as through a glass tube

I turn around
NOTHING/NO ONE/
just my books/prints/same as ever
the empty wicker chair/
newspapers scattered around/
the typewriter
the fistful of keys/

NOTHING ELSE/NO ONE
                                    and yet: I am certain:
there is someone here in my room
                                    THERE HE IS NOW
translucent as ether/
leaning against the bookcase/
                    spines now and again flickering through/
            as that violet light shimmers/
                    from somewhere within

now he selects a volume of poems
by li-tai-pe
leafs it through
sits in the wicker chair: reads

I keep watch for awhile/as he sits there
then
bend back again over my poem
                                    meantime
the rain outside picks up its pace
and drums on the rusty tin
can of a roof

half-past life

wreathed in
       wild laurel
          & stung round with wounds
             I rise from the flood

meteor showers
scattering behind
          as I spin off
              into ever-new orbit

the vector snaps

blind to the laser-flash
             & bursting of stars
       I tumble
         weightless

cold and indifferent the milky way

in wonder
receiving me
             GOD

LH 422 MUC/FRA

next to the munich-riem airport
                        as the crow flies eight hundred meters
lies the galdafing cemetery

I often stroll over there
        when I'm between flights
                        due to: flight delayed
                        due to: fog
                        due to: strike and/or
                                        cargo-bay jam
:

drifting among the headstones
                as aimless as a pinball in play
THERE SHE IS:
                she:
                        from behind
                        as she bends down
                                planting forget-me-nots
                                        on that fresh grave
HER skirt
        catching itself
on the concrete
    as she straightens

                                :

                        HER skirt
                        black/blue/black
                        the feathers
                        of a raven
                fluttering
                    among
                the stones

WHILE
    she
        gets
            to her feet
                :
                  & SHE: there she stands now
                     in her white satin slip
               & black nylon stockings
THOSE INSANELY LONG LEGS
                    there she stands
               at the grave of her man

a strange vision//she
            as she
        twists herself round/is anybody looking
      her face as pale as the sky
        & eyes welled in her sorrow
      twenty-one at the most
        a bird-like figure out of as fairy-tale
          black/lilac/white

and now
    hip shift right
    hip shift left
       :
         one quick tug
      & her skirt once again
        back in place
then down she kneels
    I watch: as her body crooks
        shivers
          clutching at earth & stone

for an instant I envy the man
beneath the mound of fresh roses/lilies/carnations
twenty-seven years young
      crushed in a cycle crash/
         dead of blood cancer/
       perhaps lung disease

IN ANY CASE
                    forty years too soon
                          for his wife
now getting up
weary & worn as a flower trod underfoot
&
moving on past not a word
                    &
                    then I read on the grave there before me
                          chiseled in stone
                               glistening/silver on black

        A GOD UNDERSTOOD IS NOT GOD

                          &: your attention please
 :
LUFTHANSA FLIGHT 422 TO FRANKFURT NOW BOARDING

memo to physicists

OK:

           in the end it's all made up of hydrogen

:

           the wing of my old vw   / / / / / / / /
           my toothbrush

           a woman's thighs

       no one argues with that -----------

BUT IN-BEWTEEN

                  between the paths of electrons
& the hydrogen nucleus
        (which you know better than I & why
          would I go you one better)

in-between is a space
so empty   even your digital microscopes
could make
nothing of

        :

        :

/ / / / / / /   that is the space
         that I need

         for my poems

HÖLDERLIN

high in his tübingen tower
                        was he mad
                                    or just
            playing the role of the madman
                                    sly enough
to survive
            mind wide & heart of the lover-swan
                beholding the ether
                                    to breathe
so be it:
            he had lived
                        and drunk upon kisses
tumbled
            the GODS

BY CHANCE

I wanted to tickle old chance
                              & we'd have it out
                    willy/nilly
            whatever the answer might be/was
                              to a question like
what is life?
              OR
                  should I/shall I rather question
what is /
        love?
            AND SO
                    I stood myself/stand myself
                              eyes good and tight
                    in front of the bookshelf
                              fumbling over the spines
                        leather/linen/paper
                        at random
                        nerves/down to the fingertips
                    tensed
                        tingling
                              eager to turn on the juice
WOW WHAT A CHARGE!!!
                        & NOW
        blindly yank down/a book/
                  arbitrarily/flip to a page: any page x
                        wherever
                        no second thought
                              wide to the old game of chance

& here it is:
                I hold
                        in hand
                              here
                                  I hold

A HISTORY OF THE WITCH TRIALS
      by soldan-heppe
                    volume 1 page 399

*"the seventeenth century practice was to burn only the most prominent
and unrepentant of witches, the contrite were mercifully offered a choice
of the axe or the rope..."*

            devil only knows
                        what that's supposed to mean

&
LONG LIVE ENLIGHTENMENT!!!

vivisession

do you know albert?
nurse mary's boy albert
eleven months/red as a lobster
                & just twenty pounds
besides illegitimate BUT
who really cares
                he laughed a lot slept a lot drank a lot of milk
entertaining himself crawling on the floor/playing with toys &
teddy bears/but most of all he liked playing with CHARLY
charly the tiniest
cuddly-cute
white
snub-nosed rat
albert loved charly/charly loved albert
the two were inseparable
                TILL DR.WATSON ARRIVED/dr.john b.watson
                      I have need of such a baby
dr.watson said to nurse mary
                one cheerfully frolicsome & whineless
          for a bit of harmless/research
                      said dr.watson
            albert is just what I've been looking for
                said dr.watson
        could be a nobel prize in this who knows
           or the rockefellers might even chip in
a few bucks
        at the least he'll amount to something your
son

nurse mary was so impressed
dr.john b.watson was a famous researcher
        at even more famous johns-hopkins university

e.g. said dr.watson
what happens
    where I to wash out his mouth with ammonia?
    HE SCREAMS
    or when I put a burning match to his thumb?
    HE SCREAMS
    or when I prick his tiny testies with a pin?
    HE SCREAMS
             and so
               dr.watson said
                   concluded dr.watson
children do not scream/because they scream/but because their
screams are triggered by something external/
nothing to do with likes or dislikes or genetics or anything to do
with things internal
        ENVIRONMENT IS ALL
and what say
said great dr.watson
       & what bet
          said dr.watson
             what bet
      that this albert
        who laughs
            &
           is frolicsome
              & cheerful
         & whineless
will whine quick enough
     when he's put to the methods of science?
said dr.watson
       HENCE
the fact he won't whine/we'll subscribe to externals alone
what this albert needs
is a small dose of fear
& once he knows fear/he will know when to whine
              said dr.watson
& then I'll have proved
why it is children whine
& the world be better & nicer & wiser than it was heretofore
for nobody's known until now: why children whine: except me

AND SO
       dr.watson snatched the white rat
              with the snub of a nose
          by the tail
             & come/albert/dr.watson said
           charly wants to play
               said dr.watson
            & albert laughed & longed for charly
     & to love him

but dr.watson
the famous researcher
       struck an iron pipe
          with an iron hammer
             a hair's breadth behind
           albert's ear
         & ripped his charly away
               so albert screamed
                    & he whined

look at that
         dr.watson cried
               albert whined
        & let his charly
           dangle again to and fro
        in front of his nose

&
yoo-hoo
albert
said dr.watson
        oh where oh where is nice little charly
          & just as albert was about to reach out
     dr.watson struck again
        iron hammer upon iron pipe
     so loud/
        that albert covered his ears
          & screamed still more & he whined
        & buried his face in
           his pillow

HE WHINES
                    SEE ALBERT WHINES
                                        rejoiced dr.watson
                    he knows fear now and he whines
                            & so that he whines a bit more
                    I'll make him fear a bit more
                            and beat a bit more on the pipe
                    hammering iron upon iron
                    & till all the world hears
                            dr.watson has discovered why it is
                    albert whines
                                    because he knows fear
                            and the fearless never whine
                    so for him I'd prescribe fear in a regular dose
        & thus
                    dr.watson hammered & banged
                            in the great cause of science
                    (and of course on no other grounds
                            and who would have hit on the thought
                    dr.watson god forbid
                                    was a sadist
                    no/dr.watson cries libel on anyone who says/
                            he's a sadist)
        so on dr.watson hammered & banged
                    a hair's breadth behind albert's ear
                    hammering iron upon iron
                    till albert trembled & cried
            just to see his chum charly
                            so in fear was he now
                    of the clang
    & never again would he play with his toys
                    & laugh as before
                    hunched lifeless & dumb
                            pale and the glint gone
                            out of his eye in his bed
        & dr.watson noted each shudder
        & each shriek
        & each shiver
                    that came with the nightmares
        & then albert turned blue/gasping for air & threw up
                    & his heartbeats grew faint

&

so that's that/dr.watson said/to nurse mary
albert has come through at last
HE HAS FEAR
how right I was that
fear springs from without
& not from within
& the world never knew that
till now
& when the nobel prize comes my way
or six dozen new babies from the rockefeller
foundation
all due to albert
oh albert will make you so proud
if you like
just dispose of him now

dance to life: 1984

NO WAY ON EARTH on my own can I stop
the nuclear build-up
daily increasing
east/west
NO WAY ON EARTH
on my own can I stop
the rivers from
spewing their toxic
guts into the seas
& the dearth of the african velt
WHILE the rainforests of amazons
are laid waste
to turn a return

NO WAY ON EARTH
alone can I stop
a lost generation
shooting death on the steps
of frankfurt/main station
unemployed fathers
battering their wives
or interpol's illegal file
on me/just in case

etc

:

BUT IN THE END NO ONE PULLS MY STRINGS
BIG BROTHER

:

to dance with you your dance of death
                                    I will come sow
                          my apple tree
                             build my house
                                          I will
                impregnable
                impenetrable to your laser-rays
                              &
                             mumbo jumbo
THERE WILL I COME TO LIVE
                come to dance my own dance
                      come to laugh & to pray
                             come spin my own web
                      of comfort & of joy

and
may ALL
come to confusion
            become I irresolute

remembering george whitman

that was his life
back then
george whitman
in his bookshop/
    SHAKESPEARE & COMPANY he called himself
on the left bank/notre-dame
cross the way
           like a rodent
nose deep in the trash
he dwelled
there among his
        dust-gray
           dog-eared
              worm-eaten
WONDERFUL   books
        the soiled linen-covers
        worse-for-wear paper
          leather-bound some
            /
           time bestained

sex and violence
that's what people want
        he'd tell me
        /
        that thin smile of his
     emerging
        out of the threadbare dressing gown /
      as he leafed through my poems
      on god & infinity
sex and violence
my dear boy
remember
    & he'd bury himself once again in his
          dusky hole

                    & I thought

                              is that all?

                                    NOW

now my old poems
lie secreted
tucked behind steam pipes
          tied three times around with thick twine
      & long since engraved in the dust
              those of the white-clouded welkin
                    & the glimmering gold set of the sun
                & the feeling: god can't be far
and
yes life has got to me
&
sex yes
&
yes violence

PARIS: *a map of the city*

in paris there is an avenue
                    president wilson
in paris there is an avenue
                    president kennedy
in paris there is an avenue
                    new york
        :
in paris is there no avenue
                    villon
in paris is there no avenue
                    rimbaud
in paris is there no avenue
                    baudelaire

            :

in paris is a petite
            rue goethe

hello dr.barnard / still with us dr.barnard?

dr.barnard is a celebrated man

he cuts out the hearts of the dead
& plants them into the living

insanity eh?

first he met mr.blaiberg
mr.blaiberg might well have lived on with his
patched-up old pump
for another three weeks
or six years
maybe
who knows

dr.barnard well he knew better

phil
said he to mr.blaiberg
I'd give you just say two more weeks
not one day more

mr.blaiberg well he winced

but with a brand new heart
phil
said dr.barnard
with a new heart you'll be able to leap up
and go for the gold

mr.blaiberg he nodded
&
dr.barnard fixed him up with a fresh-cut heart
from one of hell's angels
who'd been flying too fast
& mr.blaiberg was ready to leap up
and go for the gold

not so fast
phil
said dr.barnard
whoa! even rome wasn't built
in a day
we first need to see
if our new heart will take
& not be tossed out by
a few naughty cells

yes said mr.blaiberg

to be safe let's give you a couple of shots
said dr.barnard

yes said mr.blaiberg

and a couple of capsules as well
phil
to help our shots work a bit better

yes said mr.blaiberg

might be
slight danger of jaundice
said dr.barnard
but what's one little case of jaundice
compared with a new heart
that's going to let you leap up
and go for the gold
yes or no phil?

yes said mr.blaiberg

so until our new heart gets in gear
we need to keep you immobile
phil
we'll see you get the best room
& the prettiest of nurses
& the juiciest of steaks

yes said mr.blaiberg

the tubes & needles & drops oh that's just in case
& the probes attached to your skin
phil
& the cords
& the cables
& the scanner/controls/blood-pressure gauge
& the graph that measures the heartbeat
all simply safety precautions

yes said mr.blaiberg

and to ease the pain
phil
from the incision around your new heart
you shall have all the morphine
one could ask for

yes said mr.blaiberg

also to monitor your brain-waves
said dr.barnard
the brain here is crucial
phil
said dr.barnard
we're going to do a little
shave of the head

yes said mr.blaiberg

so the patient mr.blaiberg
he coughed
spewed up blood
came down with jaundice
& two heart attacks
& then on to severe meningitis
but yes pulling through
in anticipation
of being able to leap up and go
with his brand-new heart
for the gold

mr.blaiberg

and when a rare good day fell in-between
dr.barnard summoned a press conference and
:
you see
said dr.barnard
mr.blaiberg he's alive & he's well
said dr.barnard
& in no time he'll leap up go for the gold

& mr.blaiberg said
in no time I'll leap up
and go
for the gold

and the press announced to the world:
mr.blaiberg to go for the gold

but mr.blaiberg didn't leap up

mr.blaiberg
simply

dropped dead

the ballad of andrea lindt

andrea lindt leaned out the window
                 of her room floor 6 block C
           through the iron grating staring
                     into the sun beyond
                  swimming in a sea of blue
so beautiful
my sun
whispered she
so radiant so pure so free
                 oh how I would love you
                 how would I love and caress you
                     my glimmering god
the sun looked down
down on her window/bars/and the locks
down on her hands
         and the ghostly pale of her face

come eventide
andrea
come eventide
come thou with me
               upon my journey
           we twain shall make love
          shall love and caress
               the nightlong

and as the twilight turned dusk
and the last rays of sun
slid along the sill of her window
                andrea lindt slipped through the bars
                and out of her room floor 6 block C

the sun she embraced
to the sun she made love
loved and caressed
the nightlong
           come the sun
           she did not come again

the handmaidens of UR in chaldea

as death took their lord *the great king*
     they dressed in their festive
  diaphanous raiment & fastened
     in brooches of gold as to dance
 painting the pale of their lips
    in the red of the purple snail-shell
  eyes shadowed in the blue of
     the butterflies-blood
   enwreathing their hair
      in the gold-leaf of birch
    armbands with the leap
  of gazelles
        thus attired
beshowered in rosewater singing
   to the harps & lyres
    they lay themselves down
 in the open grave
near their king
   upon the bed of wild rushes
  in praise of their GOD
     each draining off
   their vessel of clay
  the venom
      benumbing the smile
   uniting in death before
    the earth tucked them in
 & filled up the shaft
  to the rim
entombed at the last
   & in mortar and stone
 by hands
  of the slaves

ode to fourteen-year-old junkie stella j.

she lay there stretched out
in a graceful pose of spent love
the eyes gently shut/head inclined to one side/
      her face shimmering pale
                through the web of her hair—
    still she lay there
    in what seemed a smile
  deeply immersed in the peace
      of a star-world
  millions of light-years away

the zip of her jeans was undone/a hint
of briefs peeping out like the rind of
a fresh-quartered orange

                so there she lay
                still & relaxed & still slightly stiff
                by her works and aluminum foil

the blood in the needle-tracked veins of her arm
had already congealed/as they slid her to me
in the morgue van

:

          gently I open her mouth
              shoot the rest of the heroin under her tongue
            kiss the waxed beauty of her face

:

safe journey
stella
safe journey

at the bar / la tierra / ibiza

three times tried to do away with himself
and he's not yet twenty —
francesca nodded in the direction of the garden door
manolito they call him here

I peer through my glass
regarding him in the smear of a mirror
over the bar
:
he stood leaning up against the doorpost
calm
cool
collected
his hollow cheeks colored deep brown
rutted like the bark of an olive
or
that corked-oak by the church
:
his long black hair draped to his shoulders
shimmering blue in the dense tobacco fumes
of la tierra
glass-pearled beads shining at his throat
amid a necklace of sea-shells
and
if I'm not mistaken
from a leather thong hung a kind of cross
made of tin —

now he opens his eyes/those huge eyes
smiles
stroking the head of the girl perched before him
on the stool

---

and he stands there
smiling/still/sunny & tanned as a child
wordless/questionless in the throbbing hammer of rock music
as late into the night
she and I
head back to our hotel
in the calle garijo on the harbor

----

the morning woke us to a sound that would otherwise
be no more than a sound of the harbor
mornings

francesca slides out of her quilt
peeks through the crack of the shutters down to
the street
                    gorgeous
                        as she is unrivaled
                    naked to the zebra-stripes
                        of the sun
her bed-warmed scent now engulfing the room
--
a sudden stillness now
outside –

I believe
this time he made it
she says

--

the dancer on the rue st.denis

98^0 past midnight
      the air thick/glued
    to the walls of the buildings
             the whores
      loitering about
              the swelling of thighs & breasts out
        you can sample the fruit for
            an ice-cold coke
                 AND YOU:
all you want to do now is
      to plunge in a tubful
         up to the neck swimming ice-cubes
      dreaming of naked cool nights
      by the sea
         stars so near you can touch
                BUT
        here you are
      with the ants in your veins
          and you know:
        you'll never get rid of this itch
          in the swamp of this night's air

AIR RIFE WITH THE STENCH OF ROTTING APPLES
      this goddamned sweltering heat
          THIS FEVERING FLESH
& so turn the bloodsucker on
      flush it all off down the drain
         & for a moment feel better
THEN:

then:
    she dances
        on the edge of the curb
            turns a circle
         swings a half-empty bottle of red
            swaying away to some
          unsung far-off tune
    NOW
      she pours
         wine over
            her head
      lapping it up
         with a grape-stained tongue
      as it dribbles down
      cheek & nose-tip
         to a gaping hole of a mouth
          & toothless
  as drowned as a sewer-rat
    this one seems
   burned-out by long days & nights
    between garbage bins
        & the gutter
   a skirt torn to shreds
     blue/gray/black
    that shabby man's jacket
    far to big
      &
     scavenged
        wherever

and she dances & dances & dances
     staggering
       spinning
         her laughter
            shrilling
       the paralyzed night
      like a knife snapped
           in half
and she dances & dances & dances
         rabid she circles
          round her mad laughter
          no one heeding her NO ONE
     as she
       now
         tears out of the jacket/strips
       like a birch splits its bark
        &
        out bursts
          her body
         that girlish body
      arms speckled across
         stained yellow & brown
      dark-blue the bruising
       all down her back
and she dances & dances & dances
       & the dogs now
          all begin sniffing
        & the blacks back off in fear
            & NOW
    she hurls the bottle
   slinging it
     rattling the roll of shutters
    that splinter
      the doll shop windows
         in shivers of light

    & she smashes
          hard to the wall
        hitting her head
  on the cast-iron gutter pipe:drain
                once
                twice
                three times
                    WINE-RED RED
                    AND BLOOD-RED RED
                        all arms & legs
                she tumbles
            over the curbstone

:

blood trickles awhile
from the nose and the lips
                & then: SILENCE
there she lies
        my st.denis dancer
                branded/half-dead/dead perhaps
                    bitchless
              to the one
                    invisible god
LIFE

the poem

it slithers out of its shell
sucking its lungs full of life
a nightshade/lip-rouge/ultra-violet ray

it springs into somersault
biting
scratching
kicking the world in the shins
&
looses itself laughing into air

slipping between books & trailer-trucks
without a sound
it is an MG
a hand-grenade
&
it explodes in the senate-house

it sours raspberry-ice
squeals with sheer delight
screws little girls
&
is sad

an artificial intelligence
a cloud of mustard-gas
it outstrips the measured speed of light

indiscernible to an x-ray scan

BUT NEVERTHELESS THERE

plotting revolutions
implanting ideologies
&!
outwitting them all
:
it slings its lasso round the moon
&
scrambles up
&
spooks the
living-dead below
face to face

II

...and not one line like another

the knife of the poet

the knife of the poet
        take that! I slit them apart
THE TWO-FACED & SMUG-FACED

               the knife of the poet
                      take that! I skin them alive
                 the know-it-alls KNOW IT ALL
                     they who know better
                             KNOW BETTER

the knife of the poet
        take that! I cut them all down
THE MORAL / INFALLIBLE / UNTOUCHABLES

               the knife of the poet
                     take that! sowing
                 nettles & thistles &
                    nightshade in the wastelands of cities

the knife of the poet
        take that! I slash my way out
of barbed wire
        prison yards / labor camps / psycho wards
     & shouting
               LET THEM ALL OUT

               the knife of the poet
                    I take it between my teeth
             so all can see:
                 who bares the blade in his bite

the knife of the poet
        flashing its edge to the sun I send
     signals deep into space

LONG LIVE THE FREE…LONG LIVE THE FREE…

the manhattan telephone book

there it lies before me

one volume
NYNEX
A to Z

three and a half million subscribers
    crammed together into 999 pages of fine print
I'VE GOT THEM ALL ON THE LINE

/ / / / / / /
AARMANN alec 683-9738
        to
        ZZZYADOTTE archimedes 421-34230
                 / / / / / / / /

real flesh & blood
with the sweat of their brows
      & sweet sweat of love
living & laughing
   scheming & dreaming
     loving & longing

& black & white & yellow & red

*& john got the mumps & patsy got an abortion & richard has joined
the marines & shlomo is broke & cheng's breeding spiders & sheila
she spanks her clients & alex is jogging the park & luigi's little dog
has the trots & sue buys the silk lingerie for juanito*

MEANWHILE

harold was robbed for the third time at forty-second & ninth
    & ann finally got that columbia part
        & the boys at procter & gamble
           have a new-improved bleach for your mom

&&&&&!!!
not one line like another!!!

        LEMME GIVE YA A HUG
           ALL YOUSE PEOPLE
LEMME GIVE YA A HUG
&
KISS YA DA KISS A DA WORLD
       I LOVE NEW YORK!!!

central park NYC
11:13 local time

no kids bawling today
  no dogs barking today
    no love-birding today
no gay-boys today
  no hustlers today
    no muggers today
&
 of course
 no policemen
        today
&
  no blaring
     ghetto-blasters
        today

JUST
this milky drizzle
    seeping damp under the skin
drifting out of the melancholy november-sky
of new york
today this nameless tuesday
WHERE
the cats hole themselves up in oildrums
today
where
no one no one would put up with anything
today

:

WAIT OVER THERE!?!
way over there by the boat-pond

56

                              I see him
                the 5th avenue roast-chestnut vendor
as
he
parks / un
        dis
        turb
        ed
& laughs to himself
        in his white apron
    &!
      what the hell
                who/cares/TODAY
as he helps
himself
        to a coke:can
in broad
  daylight

EMPIRE STATE BUILDING

go ahead & spit over the rail
                go right ahead
grinned the guard
        through his teeth
the spit
        never lands
                down below
    the spit
        never lands
                on anyone
                        down below
he grinned
:
nice
    to know that
I said
        &
landed one on his wart-of- a-nose
                                I just felt
somehow
like spitting on
someone
today

11:56   worn to the heel in the greasy chrome-black
night-air of new york
         cheap plastic shopping tote tucked underarm
watertight
      rainproof
          smoke-free
environmentally-safe/biodegradable/self-disposable
        stuffed-full ready to burst
with
    POETRY/
      RECORDS/
         songs & nonsense rhymes
from UNDERGROUND
           and! UPPERGROUND
yes & most of all a couple of back issues
       of black mountain review
        & hudson river anthology
   & ACID
      &
     yale lit magazine
& FUCK YOU
    +
      the unmuzzled ox . . . .
. & hart crane
. & old charles olson
. & 2/e cummings
    and OOOH! what a haul:
creely/ginsberg/ferlenghetti/f.O'hara & etc

a priceless 24-carat tiffany treasure
        assembled under
the cold watchful eye of security in three
lightning-fast hours
     at DOUBLEDAY BOOKSHOP
5th avenue & 57th street / NYC

/ /

11:57   thus weighed down
                    I wander up/down
                                    &
                                    across
5th avenue
                    like a submarine
                                    navigating
the graphite-gray gutterstreams
                            on past the fountain
heading
            north toward the guggenheim museum
yeah! sure why not! might just amble through
central park if it suits me
                    the damp night-mist fogging
my brain up with typeset & black printers-ink &
hayfever to boot
                    AND SO
what the hell
                    drizzling wet/dribbling wet
&
    joe the cab-driver's advice
                        no way STAY OUT!
it's crawling with scum
                        stoned-out hopheads
        black faggots
                        & worse far worse
and NO! not in the fog and at night
                            through the park
ah well! the same old wives-tale
                everyone here knows it
                    the hotel doormen
                        the hookers
                                the joggers
AND! of course the police
                            BUT who cares

  :

who or whom's going to bother me
              in these worn out old jeans
& baseball-cap
        & shopping bagful of records & poems
from doubleday bookshop
                that no one could smoke
or drag into the dark
         for a poke
                    / / / / / / / / / / / / /

:

11:59   DAMMIT NOW!!!!
                   for instance
                    those guys there
          the missing link between
             the orang-utan
            & neanderthal
               :
                  close on
my heels
        zig-zagging through the foggy-mist
      like a
          drunken banana-boat
/ / / / / / / / / / ===================================

00:00   one on one
         with a crooked grin
       teeth as tame as a shark's
as now he
         warmly
           brotherly
             calmly
               brotherly
slings his hairy arm around me
              towering over me
& embracing me
         like a steam-shovel
00:01   'got somethin' for me — man?!'

I see
                    I see it clear
          as my ass
                         squeezes snug
          as a bug
                         holy shit...
     just keep your head
                    don't panic now
          still no switchblade stuck in your throat
                         & the shopping bag's
                    still in your hand
                         & —
00:02   so I say
                    (just to stall him & maybe buy time
          & why not just tell him the truth?)
          'oh man'
                    I growl
                         'I got somethin' for ya'
                                        snort I
          &!
               reach into the shopping bag
                              with the bulging
                    mysterious
                         and most promising
                                   CONTENTS
                                               :

00:03   'whatcha got?'
                              showing the rotten lattice-work of
                    his teeth
                         /
                         smothering me in the reek of
                    his breath
          'whatcha got?'
                                   ?????????????

62

00:04   "I gotcha a poem"
                      I blurt out
                          I force out
                              I brazen   :
and it must have rung true
           yes! convincing!/real!/big-as-life:
short-circuiting all contradiction
                so to speak
                      &
                            dead bang
FOR:
suddenly
              like I'd flashed a police badge
          in his pockmarked mug
                    he drops his teeth
              the flesh-curtain rises
                      'ya got me a poem'
he grunts
              'ya got me a poem'
                    he stammers
                        he gapes
&!
        takes his shovel of a hand from my shoulder
            for an instant flashes the whites of his eyes
&
        vanishes quick-as-a-wink
                  into the wilds
            of central park
  :
00:05   slowly un-squeezing
    my ass
    resumes
    full
    bloom

THE SACK

in the vw-garage over there
                between the hydraulic lift &
        the carwash
                & three weeks ago
            the boss strung up the sack
                            block & chain
        a three-hundred pound weight
                    a yard and a half long
                & a good thirty-six inches across
        looking more
        like an overstuffed punching-bag
patched together from old tires
            & filled up with inner-tubes/
                        busted springs/rust-eaten
                    mufflers/exhaust pipes & junk
            & wadded with filthy black rags/
                            soaked in oil

strung/dangling from a steel-stranded cable
overhead

:

      the kid broke his wrist on it monday/
            nasim the turk first stepped a good distance
         back/before letting him have it/so hard
            it hit the roof & tore the compressed-air cables
      achim of body & fender
               worked him over/
                    till his fists drew blood:
                          but man it felt good
        schuler the bookkeeper stood to one side
             with a sick little smile WHILE
         helga the stock clerk stroked the raw flesh
               & sighed & thought god-knows-what
      christina the receptionist
            displayed the most love slitting him open

the boss grinned

he'd struck his truce

the coke-can

at the bottleneck
        right/where the road divides/crossing the A 66/ /
            as you pass deutsche bundesbank
            in the post of the guardrail

                        now in its fourth year
                            sticks a coke-can

somebody reached out & wedged it
                    ....
at first
    still brand-spanking red/white/red
        shiny new in spite of the rain
            amidst the gray of the asphalt &
                            gray of the steel
            like some stray-blown poppyseed

        one year gone lacquer cracked
    color yellowing under the rocksalt of winter
        & yet: whenever the sun shone
            the faded skin flared once again
                red-hot
                    & flashed its mother-of-pearl
            like an oyster

the rust
        came with the third year
            & came all at once both
      inside & out
              slithered over the asphalt
        crept up the guardrail
             & driving past
         you could have sworn: it grew hair/
            algae & dark lichen moss:
        the first signs of life

     now the metal's corroded
        dandelion/milkweed & wild oats
   have sown themselves in
            god-knows-how/
       blossoming up
         a kind of garden of eden
    in the making
        in the midst of asphalt & steel &
      deutsche bundesbank

....

come summer
    I'll keep a bottle of water
        at the ready under the seat:
     let the dog-days come!!!

heaven forbid:
my little herb-garden between the rails of the A 66

go to seed

FRANKFURT/MAIN - *northwest*

everyday the old lady shuffled
          (thomas-mann-ring 146 8A)
down the stairs & around the lift
and
     /down
        /the
           /whole
              /eight
                  /flights
                      /to
                         /her
postbox
forever empty
      except for the coupon circulars
from the corner supermarket
                                   &
                             sale specials
at the jiffy-carwash
             ------------------------------ THEN:
one lovely sunday
      it was warm & a seventeenth
she struggled into her coat
with the violet design
                laid on her rouge
& took a taxi to the main post office
& joined the long waiting line at the window
& sent off a telegram
               old lady frankfurt-northwest
thomas-mann-ring 146 / eighth floor / ring twice
&
    went for a coffee at krantzler's
                     & a second
&
   rode the mouse-pale orange subway back//last stop
NEXT POST won't they all be surprised

frankfurt / freedom / frolic

the bhagwani brood
          orange/pink
                   lilac/lavender
                           rosy-lip/red
flaunt their anti-violence
like a french kiss
                  banners & slogans dance
                     in the sun
                         &
                     kids sing & sway

LIVING
LAUGHING
LOVING
      &
         freelove
            &
               peace/love

in the leafless branch of a chestnut
a balloon tangles ensnared/blossoming *blue-violet*

        the police squad
           circling artfully round
        on their BMW's
           white/olive/white
        in their uniform leathers
           oleander-green

a paper streamer
              soars heavenward
                        poppyseed:red

it's springfall
in frankfurt

the mosquito

that goddamned mosquito
                              hissing around in the air
                    invisible —
                              now his racket
                              breaks off
no doubt lurking
              in a branch of that filigreed fig
        or
          secured in
                      the folds of my dressing gown
hatching insidious plans/
                      when and where/
                                    to stick it to me
SILENCE
:

THERE/ ALL OF A SUDDEN
                    again the nerve-deafening hum
                                        GOT HIM
                        now he's in sight/
                    got him/divebomber buzzing in low/
                                        now dead on target
                        my right flank exposed

:

            he lowers his singer out full/
                    sucks up his fill
                licking his lips & taking his time
                    tanking up
                on fuel enough for a week

:
gut-bucket of blood
he soars off
                looping-the-loop
                out through the half-open window

skyward

the steam-shovel driver

crash/slams
        the steel of the steam-shovel
ripping open the street
           :
        half an inch
       away from my head/down
                into the asphalt
:

YOU TIRED A LIVIN' OR WHAT!!!
            bellows the driver
            high/above higher-than-high
         one bound and he's out
             of his steel-glass cage
            pinning me down
     his face: deep lobster-red
     his eyes: a frog-pond green
     his lips: shivering/quivering/frothing
        BESIDE HIMSELF
           oh yes
       never mind men at work & danger & keep out

YA COULDA BEEN MASHED TO A PULP!!!
              he spits
    PULP MAN
            thrashing his arms about
    bawling
       waving his monkey-wrench in my face

                    & clear to me
                              he means business
                    struggling to my feet
                              timid now/intimidated
          never mind the wrench & men at work & keep out
                    just nod politely
this guy saved your life
                              I guess
                    even if he's coming on like a ZOMBIE
                              even if he'd like nothing better
                    than to break you in half
                                        the guy saved your life
                              & that much is certain/what counts
               respectfully I stroke
                                        the teeth of the steam-shovel
                    kiss the guy a smack
                              on his oily stub of a beard
and HE:
               stands like a figure carved out of wax
                              a helpless bundle of dynamite
          I love him/the way that he stands
                              & not comprehending the world

          MOVE YOUR ASS MAN // AND FAST!!!

                              73

fly / by night

while I scrabble/
                to thread the lines of my thoughts
it dives
      suddenly
        from behind me:
comes in at an angle
            lands short & hard
                  between lines four & five
     of my half-finished poem

:

stretches its feelers out

          rotating scanning the air-space
      storing up incoming data
            ground conditions
            outside temperature
            wind direction
    the translucent green of its body twitching
      in the light of my desktop lamp
    while it pumps itself full of fresh
oxygen
      via the system of conduits
              housed in its wings

:

NOW a reconnaissance mission
to the edge of the page
                         bounces off an
invisible wall/danger
                         change bearings
          now heading north-northwest
                                   coming down on the first
letter 'a' of the word radar in my poem
                         feelers now jerk erect
               wings flattened out
                    faceted-eyes signaling
          fantastic news to the brain:
                              rough-fibered terrain
                         luminous fathoms / pinnacles / networks
                    light-blasted craters & canyons:

while I stare at the standard white sheet
rag bond
8.5x11
littered with letters
waiting/desperate to be a poem

                    NOW it lifts inaudibly off
in zig-zag maneuver/flight patterns
no stunt pilot would venture
                         vanishing in the darkness behind
          along with the astonishing secret
                                   of radar-a
               for all twelve remaining
                    hours
                         of its life

ants

one
    fresh
        out-of-the-shell
                    ant
left to himself
is lost

  :

        two
           fresh
              out-of-the-shell
                    ants together build
              a nest

  :

ants

13th *may: oriole*

the oriole
      there not a stone's throw away
                                 squats in the grass
            digs right into his treasure
              /
               spreads wide his wings
            as if in nose-dive
catching the sunlight
in his sail-feathered black/violet/blue

suns himself
                       shuts his eyelets
                       :
                       cuddles up to the rays
          so happy
          so content
       without newscasts & forecasts
           & multi-vitamins & stock quotes &
           the scratched mud-wing of my vw
           wouldn't ruffle a feather

hey
oriole
give us dance
give us a song
      &
        let's fly
           into the clouds
               up and away

air-lift

eaves-dropping down from the tv antenna
dangles
     the precariously thin skein
               of an inchworm

stop & go
     like a trapeze-artist dizzied by heights
spinning down
          JUST
in the nick
I puff him away
from my teacup
in which otherwise/
       dead certain/
          he'd drown

:

now
swinging out wide
past the edge of the table
spools himself down
to the depths --
       --
      --
     --
    --
   --
       -- landing soft
         as a snowflake
       on a sandstone slab

bend squinch together/extend//bend squinch together/extend
a real-live chinese lantern inching forth
darkgreen//lightgreen//darkgreen//lightgreen

van/
ishing
        head:
        first
                in the next fissure
                                between
                                lichen & moss

:

DON'T ASK ME
what I've beamed in to land
                        BUT I'd bet you
someday
will turn
will turn
someday
                into an emperor moth/flaring-up red
if but/
it survive the next/
acid-rain

fender / bender

meanwhile
　　　　the windshield wipers of my car
　　　　　　　swish their semi-arcs
　　　　　　smearing my windshield
　　　　　　　　in non-transparent streaks
I see HER out the lefthand window
　　　　on the sidewalk across the street:

　　　　　　in the snow turned slush
　　　　　　　　　she drags the sled behind
　　　　　　　while her little prince
　　　　　　　　　　clings on fast
　　　　WHOOPS!
　　　　　　now he plunges
　　　　　　　　　dog-paddling
　　　　　　　into a puddle of ice
　　　　　　off swims his poodle/
　　　　　　　　　　　　cap
　　　　　　　SQUEAL like
　　　　　　　　　a pig:chubby chops/
　　　　　　　flushed
　　　　at once she/SHE'S
　　　　　　THERE
　　　　　　　brushes him off

kiss:

      smack:

            bubble:

                  gum

   & off they go

      little prince blows

    a huge balloon that bursts

           plastering pink

       across his face like

          an ink blot

  & whooping

     & laughing

   & now she's laughing too

     beneath her fox-fur beret

  & I

GODDAMMIT//////

   engine chokes

     car stalls

   in the midst

    of the crossing

   oncoming traffic

                CRASH!!!!!

RED LIGHT / first day of school

stopping for the light
        I see her in the rearview mirror:
at the curb behind & jumping up and down
      through the rush-hour traffic //
                      her skirt
billowing up each time she jumps
      a parachute
      and pair
        of
      knee-
      stockings
      in mid-air//////
laughing she murmurs to herself
AS IF all the world were
hers alone
:
just like the backpack
&
the bagful of gummy-bears in hand

GREEN

ice-poem

32 degrees outside
                & ice-crusted
the magnolias

the magpies
devouring the buds
by the dozen
                what you get
for wanting to
blossom too
soon

on the perils / of writing poetry

SHE was/is still:
> a young poetess
>> somewhere up on north seacoast

>> when one encountered her
>>> it was
>>>> like bathing in the froth
>>>>> of roast-chestnuts

> or
>> uncovering the first
>>> ice-crusted cherry
>> blossoms of spring

:

I'd given her a volume of my poetry / & forgotten
both long since —
> *TILL*
>> *suddenly*
>>> *two years later*
>> *in the mail*
>>> *a postcard from her*

YOUR POETRY MAKES ME PUKE /
I CHUCKED IT OUT WITH THE TRASH

:

                              BACK THEN
      I remember--
            her verse
                  the splinted-glass of her soul
            as delicate
                  & fragile
            as the wings
                  of a glass-blown moth

            she'd hawk her poems
                  at the book fair
            hand-written
                        on scarlet-red bond
                  like a flower-girl
                        & at 50 pfennig a piece —

:

my god
      it gives me the chills
what luck
      that I
            live in frankfurt
                        in the year 1987
            & not in st.petersburg
                        anno 1767
            the empress —
                        WOULD HAVE SEEN ME BURNED
                  along
                        with my poems

death / the beauty & me

on my way to the bus
I met death face to face
the sixth of last june

he'd spiffed up for the occasion
   silk tux/patent leathers/black sapphire studs etc
  ralph günther mohnnau
   says he
     time has come
     your time has come
     take your choice: car crash OR plane crash
     OR drowning in
       the sea off cape nono

is this a challenge/I ask
choose your weapons/says he
ok
say I
que sera sera...
     I was playing for time
     meaning somehow to stall him
fifteen minutes
says he
   & seats himself next to the white-faced beauty
     who sat awaiting her bus
clear to me: I had to get round him somehow
I've so much love of life & the sun
   & the way he just sidled right up/
    with his choice of some damned misadventure
     simply just out of the question
     hey death
       :

     say I
      : what's first to go
  my write hand/
   or my belly-button/
    or perhaps my left ear?

death grins: I'll have it all

you're welcome: soul included/I asked & moreover: what of
the SPIRIT/you can't just rip that out lickity-split from under
the nails AND: SPIRIT & SOUL they're immortal
so for you nothing here
                        FOR THAT death wasn't prepared
I'll have it all/says he
        but his voice had the scratch
                        of an old phonograph record
hey death/
        say I/
                is this some kind of joke/what's mine/go ahead
            rip it all out: my hair & my toes &
                the skin of my teeth be my guest
BUT as far as the soul goes
                    &
                    the spirit:
        you're up the wrong tree
                & till that's settled between us
                    no ripping & no choice of weapons
& what's more: what good is a bunch of my dried up old bones/
a shriveled-up liver & these gray hairs on my chest:
three days at most
        I'd rot to the core/I'd ooze sludge & slime
                & hell would stink to high heaven
THAT DID IT:
dead bang: now I had him ace up
                                STILL
                somehow I pitied him
            sitting helpless there at the bus stop
            & the sweet scent of beauty engulfing him/
                as she smiles at him/
                                toys
                with her thigh
                                        :

that's the last straw
up he jumps
old death/stalking away
BUT
catching hold of his sleeve
hey brother
say I
no hard feelings
say I
you win some/you lose some
I say
        so what say we shake hands and be friends
be a sport
& then waltzed him into the nearest
             applewine pub
          &!
                caroused till soused to the gills
                come the dawn

a poem slips by the psycho-ward

YOU/
     said petra/
           as if she were addressing the milkman/
             you could read some of your poetry
            to our psychiatric ward/
               we really could do with
                     something novel
                for a change

:

SO
saturday afternoon/I read
from my poems
            to the mad
              & half-mad
                & perhaps not-so-mad

      & I read them one
         & they gape at me/
     as if I'd come from outer-space
    & I read a second
       & they slouch in their folding chairs
           eyes dumb/benumbed
                  : lifeless
    & I read a third
      & one of them giggles
        & wriggles his tongue
               ALTHOUGH
    there's nothing to giggle about

&:
THEN
ALL OF A SUDDEN
         as if someone threw the switch
      they're all giggling & sniggling
          tearing their hair/baring teeth
             the mad
              & half-mad
                & perhaps not-so-mad
     & by the fifth poem
        springing up/stamping & screaming
            chaos unleashed
   & one of them slings a chair
     through the air
        &
          another grabs a nurse
           by the throat
  & ALL HELL BREAKS LOOSE
mad & half-mad & godknows-how-mad
    vs.
    warders & nurses
    at frankfurt psychiatric
TOTAL INSANITY!!!!!!//////
      how they let loose at each other/
          smash up everything in sight
       & the wood splinters
        & fragments let fly
      & now one rips the window-bars
     free & flings them into the maelstrom
& there: I stand
   my poems in hand
     & I've the impression:
   it's all so goddamned real/
      one would think: fassbinder was shooting
    the gunfight at OK corral
      & all for a handful of poems

what's more
            the mad & half-mad & surely-not-mad
                        just let it all go/as they
                turn on the taps/and let fly

                                        BUT

        for me I think best/
                    find the quickest way out
                before the leg-of-a-chair runs me through

:

THEN
            I hear her voice
                    & her hair tumbling loose across her
                institutional: gray/blue grays
                            & she shows me a palm-sized
                        notebook
                            red/blood-red
    I am ophelia
    the poetess
    thy beloved
                    read thou my poems

                & I look her in the face
                    & I think:
                        she the madonna as you've always
                    envisioned

AH BUT: ophelia
            for a madonna
                    you are
                        too young
                            just a child

& I leaf through her book/
       through illegible scribbles
             & crazy-quilt symbols
& I say: what lovely poems you've written/ophelia
    & she says: please write one of yours in my book
& through her eyes/within
       shine two eyes out at me
& through her voice/within
        there speaks a voice to me
from a world/light-years away
OPHELIA: who art thou? wherefore art thou?
OPHELIA: what wouldst thou of me?
           & I write across the last page
            "thee I love"

THEN
the shrill of alarm-bell
& twenty warders storm in
& show the mad & half-mad & not-mad
    what sanity is
          & two drag ophelia to the floor
             & struggle her out

& THE HEAD SHRINK ROARS:

        YOU/with the poems
        don't ever pull that again!!!

encouraging / young poets

with your poems
           you'll never outshine an onassis
                         & for your sake no john wayne
                 will blast from the hip

                              AH BUT

you'll have jackies galore to suck on
           your toes

&

   la-otse to pass you his flute of bamboo

the bus driver

MEANWHILE/while
the passengers out/in the driving rain/frozen in the ice-cold/
line up at the shuttered doors of the bus
PALMENGARTEN/HAUPTBAHNHOF
                                        inside HE
                                                unwraps
                                        his breakfast
                                                from the waxpaper
                        spreads it out in anticipation
                between steering column & dashboard
                        hand-picks a tomato out of the
                                        briefcase pours greenish
                                coffee into a paper/
                                                        cup
leans over the front wheel & chewing
                                mouth open wide
                        surveys the world from the throne of
                his driver's seat
                                heat up to full

:
those outside
the closed doors of the bus
                waiting/shivering/freezing
                        umbrellas & without & whatever
still seven minutes till scheduled departure & RAIN/ice-rain
getting worse as HIS salami nearly slips
                        off the bread
                                BUT
                                        deft maneuver
                                                of the hand
                back in place
                        sandwiched between half-eaten
                                slices like a rare
                                        postage stamp

SO
        while outside I/we outside/outside I
                slowly get drenched through to the skin/icing-up
YES!!!!
        HE plays
                with the headlights
                        & the tail-lights
                        & the windshield wipers
& now honking away at his
        tri-toned horn giving me
                        gooseflesh down to my toes
                as he chortles away to himself
                        self-satisfied/
                                self-righteous/
                                        secure
his mind on his old lady/dripping the stuff straight
into the parakeet's water to guard against ringworm that
                        now he demolishes
a fistful
chomping up chunks in his
        orang-utan's bite like
                        a sawmill the last
scrap of salami & tomato mashed-up together & ALMOST!!!
waxpaper too
                &
                slugs his green coffee down
        like a cold beer
                        HE stuffs the rest of his breakfast
  in the briefcase/licks his fingers/
                picks a few crumbs off his pants
&
NOW: now!!!
now's the time: for him to push the button: that
opens the doors
&
lets in/those outside/
his drenched-to-the-bone & soaking-wet & snow/frozen
                                        passengers
into the glow of his bunker

but
       first a look at himself in the rear-view mirror
             & a good scratch at the crotch/fish
          a tomato-seed out of the carnivorous: bite
AND!
      he presses the button which
      opens the door at the rear
               where of course nobody's waiting
in this goddamned rain/turned sleet
              ALTHOUGH

regulations observed/
one hundred percent right
given mothers with children & handicapped & wheelchairs
even if no
mother
&/or
children
&/or
handicapped are waiting

NOW:!!
  the front door slams back
          doing its best to squash one of us
      & zip up the steps I go/
            handing him a ten mark
note &!!
       AND!!! *no don't you have change!!!*
           he snorts at me/reeking of venom
oh! just had a flash
       he might call the police or his union
     I just might be a thug-on-the-run
        might I
           might I
             might I not...
you wait there till I can make change!!!!
he hisses through yellow teeth/
       like a worn picket-fence
     sticking from his gums

                              & I squeeze to one side/wedged
                    in the folds of the accordion-door
                              between drenched coats & umbrellas
                    & the stench of mothballs & mildew
and then
!!!!!
I CAN'T BREATHE ANYMORE/going to puke

                    LET ME OUT OF HERE!!!!!

and I elbow my way out of my prison

back into the ice & wind/into FREEDOM

                    I let the snow thaw on my face

                              I inhale/devouring the damp cold drops

rot in that hole
you poor stupid
bus driver
go to hell!!!
&
that's all
you're good for anyway

AT/forty-two

specialist in lung disease/chairman of the league of fine arts/

one of the best tennis-players in town

HE dined at the finest clubs

read schopenhauer/heidegger
adored beethoven & mahler
                 & his four children: his wife
doe-eyed/long-limbed/spiritual/KENZO & GUCCI

                     everyone envied him
                     his house on the park
                     his yacht at port grimaud
                     his collection of egyptian clay arts

his fortune seemed consummate
but to speak of it: silence

              ONE DAY HE VANISHED WITHOUT TRACE

they searched/but in vain
crack detectives/at a loss

NOW THE WILD RUMORS
BEGAN

one claimed to have seen him
                on an old rusty trawler
        off santa lucia

another maintained
        he now had a beard & was painting
like a madman

                many imagined:
                        he was hatching some coup d'état

but the state still wouldn't rule kidnapping out

worry increasing with each day/
                                as to his whereabouts
                the press kept the story front page

:

NO ONE
hit on the thought
that he'd just had enough of it all

&

simply
dropped out of
sight

PICASSO

vauvenargues 30 may 1982

I squeeze myself
                through the local police barricade
        unhook the iron chain across
                the drive to the chateau EVEN
        the wrought:iron fence could be scaled
WERE IT NOT
                were it not: for the surly concierge
OR RATHER: could be but for the snarling fangs
                                of the german shepherds
                                        / / / / / / / /

DON'T TROUBLE YOURSELF
                        laughs picasso & pulls
                me through the iron rails
                        and into the garden
                as if made of AIR
off we trudge/trudge
                through the damp wet grass
                                up the front steps
                                of the chateau
            picasso points back at the lawn
                that's where I'm buried / my bones / there
            beneath the MOTHER EARTH sculpture
only now I notice
he's smoking a cigarette/the smoke indiscernible
                STILL steady drizzle
        but above the hills of sainte victoire
                the sun peering between clouds black/black/violet
                dipping their edges in glistening light
        a rainbow spanning across
                        the corner towers of the chateau
        blue/silver/yellow/red
let's sit down
says picasso

100

& we seat ourselves on the well-trod steps
                        by the main door
                its paint peeling now
        & giving off a scent of an oak-bark's
                dew-drenched moss

for awhile we talk of women & bullfighting & *your memorial//*
        retrospective in new york
                                I say
                                was a smash hit
                                                I say

the waiting line was six hours long/ the
scalpers getting a hundred bucks in the end
on the street
                I hate retrospectives
                        says he
                        retrospectives are for the dead
                                he says
I'M STILL ALIVE
        and his eyes fire up like a volcano
                                /////////////
up there in the clouds
                d'you see it
        my mandolin?
                he asks me/asks he
                                I
                see nothing/not in the
                slightest see I
                                        EXCEPT:
                clouded ice-floes/white-gray: white
        WAIT NOW/now I see it clearly/
                        swirling like a leaf of holly
                in a windstorm:
                        high up above
                                the mandolin
this way
        calls picasso

101

& dives into the rainbow/
in the midst of the foaming lilac/swimming
through grains of red/into the algae green
coming up orange/yellow/white:light
and snatches it:
HIS MANDOLIN
& strums its strings
& his eyes aglow
& his voice booming out
as he sings an old flamenco
out of his presentpast

SHALL WE DANCE
cries he
& we take one another by the hand
skipping from cloud to cloud
through the misty mountaintops
swinging & swaying
& NOW:
hold on fast
he roars

&

we plunge
head:long
to earth
thirty-thousand feet
through the liquid sky
weightless
as hang-gliders
& I crash in the grass
WHILE he
playfully breaks his fall
in the headwind
and:
come as often as you like
I hear him cry as he
swings himself
up & into a sunbeam

: I watch after him
as he slowly fades from sight/
                          soon in:visible
                first his limbs
                      then his face
                            then his eyes
                                  last of all
                                        his eyes

KEY WEST / SLOPPY JOE'S / *then now*

the same old flies the same
&
the cockroaches

                    same
                    old whiskey's the/
                    same
                    &
                    same ceiling-fan

everything else is something else
since then
hemmingway too
no longer the same
                    he slouches
                        at the bar
                            slurping milk & honey
                    hands a-quiver
                        &
                            nobody notices

no-smoking / poem

all smokers
pollute the environment
pollute the environment
and you murder children
and you murder children
                    you get put TO DEATH

:

AND SO!!

let's just drag the old GUILLOTINE
out of the reinickendorf museum
&
set it up in the marketplace
&
get those heads: ROLLING
&
let blood

& give the kids something new
*   to kick about!!!*

III

sheddings

___*rgm*_____

the tides of love

all life has its hour
& all love in its time

:

a time for pillow-fights & a time for pillow talk
        a time to kiss & a time to bite
                a time to sow & a time to reap
        a time to let go & time to hold fast

a time of lust & a time of fear
        a time to be jealous & a time to forgive
        a time to flee & a time to pluck thorns

a time to tear & a time to mend
        a time to scratch & a time to caress
                a time to dance & a time to weep

        a time to hurl stones & a time to hoard stones
                a time to cry out & a time to be still

an ebbing of loss & a tide to come home

love-poem

it is not your hands
nor that you breathe
no not your lips
                in the folds of my skin
                nor your hair is it
                your voice not
                your eyes

                :

                it is

                :
                that I fall
                        splintering
                like glass
                        to the floor

                & you pick me up
                fit me back in place
                        piece by piece
                                with a smile

memories of b

those the irretrievable things—

               the crystalline light of the sun
         that awakened us
             early that morning
          the shadow-play
              on the curtains
         & pillows
        the tumbled mess
          of our clothes
             on the floor
        the scent of your nape
            your breath on my cheek
        as constant as
            waves on the sand
    as you fell back asleep
              for a while
         beneath the tangled reeds
              of your hair

:

the silence ringing
    the peace of the oncoming day
  untouched
      by the departure of hotel guests
you and I
:

to say
       I love you
as superfluous
as speaking of the sun
on that morning
             it simply was there & shone &
         a rainbow spanned across your skin
           as it splintered
        in the old-fashioned mirror
                 across on the wall

:

we lived
      timeless
         weightless
            effortless
our love held us both in suspension

as light
&
as fragile
as the morning mist outside —

:

you and I —
       that morning
           that light
               that peace

you and I

those the irretrievable things
        that bind us over the years
      white coral —
          weathering
             the reef
               of our memories

TANYA

fourteen I think/fifteen maybe
        when she hustled me for the five/down in the subway
            hungry for life
            &
            after a big mac & fries
      a horrid:homeless little rodent/snuffling about
    with her eye on a crash-pad
  & a handful of soul

:

NOW/
        slouched on the stool
            her jeans sliced to ribbons & cotton t-briefs
        from woolworth's & red raspberry–ice sweatshirt/that
              huge tongue sticking out
                  on her chest
      & the sandals/those sandals/or rather:
            what used to be sandals

:

as the soap squeezed out of her hand in the tub &
we dove for it & our slippery-wet hands played under
the water & amidst mountains of suds
for the first time she laughed —

now she sleeps/
                    drifting in her dreams of
tarzan/
          pinball arcades/
                              popcorn & cotton candy
now and then overrun by a shudder
                              she opens her mouth
                                        lips fluttering
as if something inside wanted out
                              to rid that childish soul
of some poisonous bile

:

stretched out she lies
          arms all akimbo
                    limbless
                              weightless
                                        outstretched
her legs
wide
as if buoyed
by the sea
          a nest of seaweed somewhere in between
               the neon-pale of her skin against
                              the red brocade of the spread
               the wild violet poppy of her hair
                         seeming to have no beginning no end

the fading sun
          through the yellowed curtains
                              of the hotel room
                                        streams down
                         dissolving her body
                              in a shimmering mosaic
                         of shadow & light

:

PAINTER
          would I be now
not poet

sunday morning 9:59 / streetcorner

she sits on the trashcan
   in the
       orange
          warmth of the
              SUN
a wild poppy flower
in her hair
   completely at ease
----
          her white/violet puppy
snuggles itself into her lap & yawns
----
legs thrown one-over-the-other
     she sucks on a raspberry-ice
&
   softly smiles
       :
         "wanna go out?"

sheila

she sweeps through the doors of BAR ALEXANDER
    sheathed in black patent-leather/
  her hair phosphorescent
      dangling above her hips
    like a dragnet

///// SOMEWHERE A POET IS DRIVEN INSANE /////

& the way
       with which she throws back her head/
               brushes the hair aside/
above all
     the way she moves/
         as she gets a light from the bartender:
                      NOW
she looks around
     /
       lazily letting her steamy radar sweep
    the heads in the room
& every single male
    feels somehow ensnared
         /
        all conversation stops
              for seconds

:

in profile she seems
                    an ancient egyptian temple-dancer
          out of the 18th dynasty/
                    who knows
              why in our 20th century
                              she chose to emerge

ANYWAY far and away the best whore around

& the mad poet/the one with the wooden leg/
          now slipping down from his barstool/painstakingly/
                hobbling toward her on his silver crutches

I bet
he has one hell of a night

RIAH: *or perhaps: ria*

it was like a film/at a midnight screening/
                as she sat down by me
     in the BILBOQUET
            foreshadow/fore:shadow
                    //
                  something about her
           made me uneasy/

          this EBONY SPHINX

I believe
tonight is the night
says she
:

     I didn't know what
          I just noticed
     the fallow light
         rising from her
       hands & those fingers:
           white & translucent
        as jellyfish stingers
  & HER MOUTH
         lips springing open
               SUDDENLY

         :

just stay where you are
says she

AND her tongue tongues snakelike
                              over my flesh/
                    slithering its
                              scales over me
                         sucking/slurping me up
                                        like an oyster

              AND THEN
                         screeching up from
                              the marsh/
                         the hungry iguana
&!
    didn't I say:
              smiles she
                    tonight is the night

PARK LANE HOTEL, N.Y.

I met her
by chance
at the elevators
in the lobby

        she pressed 37
        I pressed 41

she stood far corner right
I stood far corner left

        we spoke not a word
        thirty-seven floors long

as she stepped out
she smiled

                              &

        I smiled in return

lesson: what is a poem?

tonight
      say I
tonight I'm going to
          get plastered on
                  poetry –

how
do you get
plastered
on poetry
          sarcastic she
             this I've got to see –

then you sit
      next to me
say I
   & catch me as
          soon as you see: gravity
      take over

PUNK'O'LOVE

with her red:red string-mop of hair
     studded spikes on her shoulders
          &! the silver safety-pin stuck
      through her earlobe/
           the naugahide-leather gear
        de rigeur –
SHE was really something else
            even the bike-chain round her hips
      which she insisted on wearing the whole time
        and then: THE RAT
             the sewer:black gutter-rat
          scuttling over her neck/
       shoulder/breast
     while she sucked on its tail
         like sipping a strawberry shake
         through a straw

oh man
I thought
ralph günther mohnnau / philosoph-poet / WHAT NEXT??!!
:
     her pubic hair half-shaved away/
        dyed half-shades of holly-leaf green
              :

ANYWAY
     I had it made

BUT FOR/but for:

for that damned snake
she'd had tattooed up
and down
slithering out of the furred undergrowth
gleefully twisting itself
round her navel
coiling up in the end
round her breasts
envenomed fangs viciously bared
jaws stretched ready to fasten
in her left nipple

:

as her skin burst open beneath me
breasts mushrooming
swimming////slapping beneath me
like water-swamped lilies
ALL OF A SUDDEN
the snake starts snapping
at me
eyes scenting out
& now!: lashing/zap
straight for the jugular!!!!!
I leap off my henna-haired love
rats/spikes/chains/safety-pins/
ok by me
BUT
come to snakes
baby
count me out
baby
there I'm as thin-skinned
as a dragonfly's wings
& I've no tooth for sweets
baby
& pythons
once bitten twice shy

stewardess academy

the cast/aluminum phallus
spits its bleached new-blood into the ballroom
WALDORF-ASTORIA
                              :
                         LUFTHANSA INTERNATIONAL
                                        :
deep-freeze SMILES for BOEING/DOUGLAS/AIRBUS
bonbons stowed
        newspapers stowed
          tomato-juice stowed
              chicken-breasts stowed
                cigarettes stowed
              baby bibs
          band-aids
        air-sick bags
      ashtrays check
neat-as-a-pin
:
LONG LIVE THE JET-SET GENERATION
trilingual: coffee/tea
or/in any language: me
) TAIL
                              COCK duty free
) PIT

: FASTEN YOUR CUNTS PLEASE
                        /
              THANK YOU FOR FLYING LUFTHANSA!!!

what the hell has poetry
to do with the printers union?

a lot: a whole lot: for example:

SCHEDULED to read my poems in münchen/munich/MUC/
scheduled to
BUT

due to printers strike/
     no newspapers were printed/
     with no newspapers printed/
      no one in munich read of my reading/
      since no one in munich read of my reading/
    the chairs sat there empty
     that clear-blue evening
      in the nymphenburg bookshop
          JUST me
there in the front row
   flying in on Lufthansa LH 969 & SHE
  my fragile/fond/fortuitous stranger
   with the transparent skin
     the intangible breasts
    & the sun-splotches under her eyes
     midst of winter

SO
the evening was saved after all

     perched on her cushion
       of rough-hewn jute
   legs a-knot in the lotus-pose
      of a buddhist monk
  I read her my poems
      WHILE SHE
while she
   fondly
    plays
     on my
      pan-pipe

SHE: she: sissi

between
       the cotton puffs & mascara
            the carousel of nail-polish:
aster:red / foxglove:blue / aubergine:mauve
           NEXT TO next
     to the eye-shadow/almond paste & mink oil
WHERE DO ALL THE MINI-PADS GO??????????
          quick spritz of breath-mint
            under the tongue
    & behind the ear
        a dab of diorissimo
WOW!!!!!
& then she rustles
    between sheets of black rayon silk
  my ivory-skinned beauty
      as metro:traffic updates
BUMPER TO BUMPER B69 INBOUND TO FRANKFURT......
......
   & the lime-green lather
      waits in the shower
   for the love streams

       of whi:te

nightmoth

sitting at my desk
naked

almost midnight now & yet still
                        sweltering in
               this heat
          sweat pearling
              on my chest
                       drips/streaking
           like fresh resin
                sticks/stinging
           between my thighs
I
filter my thoughts
          word-fragments
        foggy notions
          which might drift into
              a poem/quite a
           good poem even
                      IF:

if
  YOU/you hadn't
           risen up
              suddenly
          without warning
           & noiseless as a
                night:empress moth
& you coming warm
      from the sheets
                  smiling & as if
           you fresh
              pluck cherries
                  in passing

myriam / miryam / wow!!!

you wrote yesterday
says she
and once again
misspelled
my name/says she
sulks she
:
while/MEANWHILE
stripping
out of her
strawberrymilk/red
lace slip/
her cascade of hair
ensnared
in a bungi-band
lilac/blue/white
m y r i a m
understand
not *m i r y a m*
hear me
"y" before "i"
//
not after "i"
says she / WHILE she throws her serpentine-body
slithering over me
I'll make a note of it
I breathe
"y" before "i"
I breathe
nightshade &
thistledown
MYRIAM
MIRYAM
WOW!!!

YIN & YANG & all that

the masculine is YANG
but YANG is quick to excite
quick to expire
the feminine is YIN
but YIN is slow to excite
even slower to sate

WU HSIEN

you flutter beneath me
  breath escaping your lips
    earlobes a-glow your
        nostrils a-quiver &
     skin pearling/exuding the scent of
    fresh-cut chestnuts/that
        I love so/words
      mysteriously murmured //////////////
THIS THE MOMENT
     to stretch our desire/drawn out
        suspending it
      like the note of a bamboo-flute
   BUT
    you sling yourself around me/
      nails clawing into my shoulders/
    tongue plowing deep
to hell with yin & yang
     &
      ching & ch'i
        BANG!!!!!!!

mango-tea

damn that nurse in the apartment upstairs
                    half-past one and time for a poem
          but goddamned little bitch
                              PERFECT TIMING
          in she stomps from the early shift
               at the red-cross clinic
                         whacked-out & weary
                    of soiled bed-sheets/dead & dying
               the pox-ridden kids
          clear: what she needs is
                    a good straightening out/
          to flush off the blood & the needles &
                         the stale reek of death

:

SHE pours boiling water
                         over the mango tea-leaves
          slits open the tea biscuits
                    slips in a michael jackson cassette
& plunges into her wet-dreams
          on her rosy-pink sofa
                    volume full-blast

:

the razor-blade on the edge of my desk
quivers/flittering down like the torn wing of a butterfly
          clear: what this girl needs
                    is not tea & crumpets
                         is not canned michael jackson

BUT this poem of mine has a deadline
                          & not one single line written yet/
                 explain that to the magazine people/
who expect it by five
won't do/can't do/must do
                       OK up and ring her bell

&!
    hey/say I
         I've got a poem to write/
                        say I
                           &
                           you need someone
             to set you straight/
                   say I
             so how about: a poem in exchange
                  for aligning your soul

and she says: *how about a cup of mango-tea*
and I say: *I'm just nuts about mango-tea*
&
she smiles
         & we both settle into the cushy plush pink
& I say: *your move*
                & she doesn't' quite know
                     how/where to begin
           but then she just screws her tongue into me

                            & FIZZ-POP!!!

it's raining shooting stars
           &
             the milky way
       scatters every which way

          blue/silver : red/gold

lovers-leap

sweet sixteen
&
I forty-five
& pretty uptight
      given this twenty-nine year
  differential
        ALTHOUGH
             we knew of/chaplin/picasso/
                old goethe & ulrike/anyway
         I had this funny feeling
             in the gut
                  BUT
she just gave me a nudge
        just do it said she
      & I needed no second invitation
           & we take off
          & what can I say:
                  HEAVENSVILLE!!!

chelsea hotel

lying there on her back
                              & twisted up in the white sheets
                        reeking a bitter-sweet scent
                                          of lavender & bleach

:

SHE
    :

        the staccato of her body
    sweat in pearls between her breasts
             swept up in the down
                        of her skin

      thirst-quenched
            they burst
                trickling
            head-first
                into the depths
            like the dew
      of the cactus-plant
    sparkling now
      in the rays of the sun
    that shimmer
      off the plane passing by
                        overhead
hey where are you
she calls
DON'T YOU MAKE A POEM OF ME!!!!
                              and she slings the rainbow
                round me
                  & sets it ablaze

ALPHA TO OMEGA stop
                  HERE WE COME!!! stop
                    HERE WE COME!!! stop

NEW YORK / same old NEW YORK

& same old wet august weather
           soggy & hot & as thick
                           as an oyster-bar coconut-milk
& the same gray squirrels in central park
& the hot dog vendors & fire-eaters & streets
forever in a state of upheaval
& this
           & that
&!
AND SHE//

IN FACT she sees me right off
her face pressed against the smoky-glass panes
of RICHOUX
              ////
                           ALTHOUGH
I secrete myself in a corner/
                           enveloped
                                   /in the VILLAGE VOICE
like a sandwich
              //ALL IN VAIN//
                           : there she sits across from me

SANDY —
five years now/maybe six?
you'd simply slipped your arm in mine/BACK THEN/that sultry
july evening on central park south
                    the moist air trapped between the trees
                           & my shirt glued fast to my skin
                    & said: wanna go out?
my name's sandy/ from bridgeport & me/I'm ralph/from
frankfurt/germany & she said/
I'm eighteen & I/you're sixteen at most

& we laughed
& she stuffed the hundred bucks in her left boot
& shut her eyes tight
& I too
& it all ran like a film
& what lingers/is the memory of a gentle fragility
& the goddamned state she was in/
                    as she crept out of my room
back then in chelsea
sometime in the morning
between
three
&
four

:

NOW
there she sits in front of me/twenty perhaps twenty-one/
that's what the i.d. says & her face screams of squalid nights/
& of days squandered & retch/stuck fast to her soul

:

wanna go out?
& her voice the same
& her fingers: long & spindly & as white/the same
& perhaps the same: that hopeless fragility
///
I'm not in the mood/I want to say
ok baby/I hear myself say
five years is a long time/sandy
just look/what's become of us
& she stuffs the bucks in her boot
& shuts her eyes
& I too

& this time she stays the whole night

IN THE PARK: *round midnight*

her red scarf
        falls loose
   about
      her
        shoulders

her
  head
     stretched
        up against
            his five
o/clock face

:

as he
    bends
      down
        over /
          her
breasts
    caressed
      in the faltering
          glare
of the neon//
   light

:

136

more
      I couldn't
discern
        in that blink of an eye
                      as I sped past them
returning home
          from some amour
other than:
          their/flashing
              radials
locked
       entwined
            in one another's
                  wheelchair

sh:it/day this thirty-first

it's july
        &
        outside the summer's letting off steam
     trousers sticking to my thighs
the dogs
        huffing & puffing
I linger
at my writing desk/NOTHING
                        coming of/over/out
d'lovely sh:it/day today
:
SURE
       martina chooses just this moment to drive by
         in her red nail-varnished MINI outside
        & that scraggly-haired/creep/next to her:
         & SURE!!!
                she claws at his neck
     WHILE HE
          fingers her pants
        with who knows what disease
        under those nails //////////
JUST LAST WEEK
        at the westend-hotel
              now I think of it /////

one touch would make her
                   squeak & squeal
                              like a toy/baby:doll
                    skin & mouth parched
             as blotting paper
                                   &
                           sand
                                     we
reflected there
in the screen of the tv
watching/as she slings those long
                         tentacles around me
              fingers clawed deep:in the bed
          head thrown to one side
                      ////////////////////
/////////////////////
then lying exhausted there / silent / SPENT

//////////////////////
AND TODAY
the thirty-first of july and
she's throwing herself at that stinking coyote/no more
              than a burned-out would-be live-wire
I FEEL
something gnaw at my soul
                   hammering at the insides of my skull
STUFF a few ice cubes in my mouth/turn
              the loudspeakers up full/kick the
          wastebasket across the room:
              a cold shower is what I need   NOW
the phone rings
              &!!SURE: it's martina
         and: she lisps: free tonight/she taunts
       and: I say: no /I say/ok I say/why not/
           & I could bite my tongue out
         for letting her get to me
                   twisting me up
                         like some rusted old wire

139

of the ibiza maidens: las salinas

they loll about beneath the noonday blue.
tangas slung about their hips with flair.
in the suntan-cream-oil-saturated air
they revel in themselves. navels out on view.

time stands still. like the sands of an hourglass.
coke bottles shimmer in a splintered light.
skin lies slick. salamanders doze. and bite
now and again at young carrion ass.

but when night falls the cells arouse
from their sun-drunken stupor. they realize
their full of carnival and blind embrace

and wildly flitting flesh to flesh carouse
laughter shrilling their black-lacquered eyes.
to wake tomorrow to a stranger place.

love story / or: the cry of the mantis

too fragile was she for his touch
too naive for his skin
to distracted for his kiss

too silent for his words
too indifferent for his love

NEVERTHELESS:
                she drank his tea &
                      ate his chocolates
                she even danced &
                      warmed herself in his bed

        HE clung to her
                helpless/at her mercy
            like a scrap of paper
                driving winds press fast
            against the windshield

                      he knew pleasure & pain
                  & so found desire in
                        his pleasure
                          & pain

TILL
the day she found: the time had come

and she fed upon his soul
as cold
        &
        un-crying

as the mantis

lea

she arches high: a snakelike swish
of hair cascades across her shoulders
a single shudder: and she erupts
thighs sucked round him like the jellyfish

tensed she waits in indolence
while green eyes taste their prey
before the beast now springs afresh
and lips seek out his succulence

deep deeper now she genuflects
her fangs now sinking
hard into his neck and

tearing wild she vivisects
HIS WARMTH: the blood and flesh
and at last devouring his lip-smacking sex

for / against b.

I sought
    tenderness
beneath your
    tongue
    :
        I sought
           warmth
        beneath your
           arm
        :
           I sought
             shelter
        in your
             womb
           :
            AH BUT

you tear away at me
like raw flesh
&
your laughter
grates

settling-up

you took me
      with the ingrained move
of an ironbender
    sliding his iron-rod
            deftly in place
   & precise to a millimeter
          in the wet concrete
                AND YET
still you wonder
child
hah
that I repay
no more
than the wage
      of an iron/
          bender

sometimes

sometimes
I'm insufferable —
      those are the days
        when you point out
       that I'm no more
         than a hickey
           on your soul

:

THEN I wish I were a painter
        swapping you like a color
           yellow-orange for dark-red
         squeezing you out
             on a slab of wood
       smearing you out
          across the rough canvas
        beyond all recognition

on the death of a love

you and me
we never had a thing in common
                            no not dreams
                                    & no wild dance
                        no nightshades
                            & poems

                    if you asked me
                why we clung so long to one another
like wet slivers of glass
                sharp-edged
                        lifeless
                                cold
looking past one another
            &
            through one another
////
                            PERHAPS perhaps it was
                    the days/nights even
                                our discussions
                        on picasso and klee/
                                kierkegaard/
                        your aversion to
                            hemmingway
                                    & freud oddly enough
    :
you with your rimless glasses there in the odeon
            that pallid smile/
                        quivering like reeds of grass
                in a japanese garden/
                            your just plain inexperience
WHILE
            the waitress maneuvered
                    her tray of tarts among
                the marble-flecked tables/black leather skirt
& YOU

                you still off somewhere taking notes
                                on schiller's aesthetics
scribbling your hand asleep

while while
                the waitress sashays over to me
                                her skirt stretched taut at the hips
                        legs thrown into play
                                as she spits you
                        a pitying glance
                                like a
                                        cherry-pit

her telephone number scrawled across the bill
////
        yes: you and me
                        and
                        me & you

:

WHEN I THINK/what separated us
                                light-years—
BUT THEN: the few moments
                that bound us to one another
                the tiny shivers
                        suddenly flashing out of nowhere
                                when our bodies let loose
                        in a murderous lust
                        your shrieks
                                wild/shrill & metallic
                                                :

                        147

we celebrated the sacrifice of our love
in blood and sweat

           and yet: these were moments but
                light-seconds in an eternity
        of lethargy & indifference
     not enough for us both
          not enough for our love

you & me
/ / / / /
then that afternoon/you came for your things/
like picking up groceries
the last of things we had in common
tossed into the trash
like yesterday's bread

      :

      the pain was short
         the taste of it
     bitter there upon the tongue
        a few days
          not more
and now:

the empty chair
the empty bed
the wrinkled handkerchief
your toothbrush there in the glass
what about all your letters?
       I stare out the window
      nighttime in frankfurt
        a few mushy stars
        clinging above the tv tower
so girl
that's the end of the story
&
fuck you too

THE VERDICT
or:
how they did it with CYNTHIA

there was an old score / that
still needed to be settled /
back then / in the sleazy
air of LA TIERRA

she came straight up to me in the park
    canvas-bag slung carelessly across her shoulder
COULD IT BE:
            I'd already met her somewhere
    & in passing
      at one of the summer jazz-fests
                OR
                  the subway?
on the tiles lower-level graffiti that someone
had scrawled
      & in toxic:green
          WE DIE OUR OWN LIFE
    &
      below
        in raspberry:neon
            I WISH I COULD LOVE YOU
    & I'd seen her next to me
          &
            said: that's not enough
      & she'd said/with a smile:
        what more could you want?

she knew she was beautiful / so beautiful / they would pay
whatever she asked

I served her wild-cherry tea
                    over crackling candis
        & as she sat down on the floor
            a few strands of hair knotting up
                        in her belt
            & as I untangled them & feeling
        her breath on my neck
                        she said: cynthia's my name
            and I knew/
                        this was more than a game

sometimes her eyes yawned wide as craters
                                OR
were they coral-reefs / there to break waves /
                        and to be scorned by ships?

I discovered/she loved paintings
                        masks & marionettes
                meandering with her through
        museums
                    &
                exhibitions
    & nights
    & nights
            we rollicked & frolicked
                        between books & pillows
                        THEN: one morning
        there
            written across the mirror
        in lipstick
                &
                inverted
'M I N H'

a thousand reflections
                in the mirror be:hind
            trailing blood/red off into infinity
        & when I asked her
                        what it meant
            she just laughed

she took her time: a long time / all in her own sweet time

CYNTHIA
>   I love you
>   I love your lips
>   as they suck fast at my skin
>   I love you
>   the scent of your nape
>   & the sweat-pearls
>   damp between breasts
>   I love your limbs
>   as they sling round me
>   burning wounds in me
>   like the silvery strands
>   of the jellyfish
>   I love the fevered jungle
>   of your thighs
>   your piercing cries
>   I LOVE YOU

/ / / / / /
that was the moment / she'd been waiting for /
as he lay there / exposed
his soul belly-up to the surface
she struck
>   *& his death came silent & swift*

151

self-portrait

the firedamp of love
had overcome me
       :

          the breath of love
          came again to revive me
:
SINCE THEN
        what I am/am not
is love
is not love

is love

_____*rgm*___

selbstbildnis

die schlagwetter der liebe
haben mich umgerissen
                    :
                        der atem der liebe
                        hat mich wieder aufgerichtet
:
SEITHER
        was bin ich/nicht bin
ist liebe
ist nicht liebe

ist liebe

_____*rgm*___

about the author

RALPH GÜNTHER MOHNNAU was born in 1937 in the town of Bad Kreuznach, Germany. First poems and articles appeared at age 14, and an interest in poetry, painting and ballet was followed by studies in English and Romance languages, with degrees in Law and Philosophy from the Universities of Mainz, Freiburg and the Paris Sorbonne. His foreign studies have taken him to Greece, Egypt, the United States and the Canary Islands, crediting personal encounters with Martin Heidegger, Alain Robbe-Grillet, Charles Bukowski, Joan Miró, and John Cage as significant influences on his creative work.

All told, he has published more than 60 volumes of his works, many of which have been translated into English, French, Spanish, Catalan, and Japanese. His poems have been collected under the titles: *RED CORPUSCLES, ANTI-BODIES, GAMMA-RAYS* and *SOWING NIGHTSHADE IN THE WASTELANDS OF CITIES.* He has written a novel, *DANCE OF THE CONDOR,* and has translated Akenaten's *SONG OF THE SUN* and *THE LOVE POEMS* of Sappho.

Beyond poetry, his creative passions extend to musical theatre and opera. He has written several libretti -- *CAROLINE* (score composed by Michael Obst, Weimar), *WENN DIE ZEIT ÜBER DIE UFER TRITT (If Time Overflow the Banks,* for the Munich Biennale, score by Vladimir Tarnopolski), and *JENSEITS DER SCHATTEN (Beyond the Shadows,* for the Beethoven Festival in Bonn, score by Vladimir Tarnopolski, Moscow). His rock opera *H – OR, THE RAINBOW JUMPERS* (score by Matthias Raue), had its premiere at the Ohio Theatre off-Broadway in 1985, directed by OBIE-Award winner Manuel Lütgenhorst. A dramatic work, *CRY OF THE MANTIS* has been mounted in Paris, Vienna, Frankfurt, and at Seven Stages/Atlanta in 1990, director/designer Christopher Martin, music by Matthias Raue.

Ralph Günther Mohnnau lives and works in Frankfurt and Ibiza (Balearic Islands, Spain).

CHRISTOPHER MARTIN is a director/designer and composer, the Founding Artistic Director of Classic Stage Company in New York where he mounted a hundred productions over the company's first eighteen years, frequently appearing as an actor. Since 1985, his work has taken him to National and State Theatres across Europe and the Far East. As a translator, he has received a Pulitzer Prize nomination (with Daniel Woker) for the Heiner Müller text of Robert Wilson's *THE CIVIL WARS* (American Repertory Theatre), and the National Theatre Translation Fund Award for versions of German playwright Botho Strauss. A designated translator of the plays of Federico Garcia Lorca, he has also rendered Rostand's rhymed verse *CYRANO DE BERGERAC*, and plays by Roger Planchon, Molière, Strindberg, Büchner, Wedekind, and Dürrenmatt. He is currently at work on a series of crime novels.

INDEX

... and drunk upon kisses tumbled the GODS

... and not one line like another

Printed in the United States
By Bookmasters